GAMES FOR CHILDREN WHILE TRAVELING

Sid Hedges

GROSSET & DUNLAP
Publishers · New York

© Sid G. Hedges 1973
First published in Great Britain in 1973 by Ward Lock
Limited, 116 Baker Street, London, W1M 2BB
All Rights Reserved
Published in the United States by Grosset & Dunlap, Inc.
New York, N.Y.

1976 Printing

ISBN: 0-448-11919-6

Printed in the United States of America

To
Maureen and Sandra,
who helped a lot

Contents

Introduction

Traveling can be a bore, or it can be fun. Most parents do their best to see that children on long journeys are kept happy and amused, but sometimes it is difficult to think of any new games to play. Both parents and children will arrive at their destination fresher when there has been some lively and controlled activity during the journey, and there are plenty of games for people on the move which can transform boredom into enjoyment.

Most of the games can be easily simplified to suit even the youngest members of the party and nothing requires any elaborate equipment. Pack a tote bag or small case with paper, pencils and crayons. Take a checkerboard and a couple of packs of cards — and include a dictionary to help settle any wrangles over word games! A flat piece of hardboard, or a tray, or even a suitcase can make a good laptable.

Have a good journey!

Watching

Looking out and around while you are actually traveling can provide a lot of amusement.

Seeing Things

Two, three, or four people can take part in this game. If still more players want to join in, they can work in pairs. Each one taking part will have his own list of things commonly seen while traveling along, and each item will be crossed out as it is spotted. In preparing the lists, take into account the area you are traveling through, so that all competitors have an equal chance of seeing the things they want.

Here are some examples of the sort of list you might compile:

A	B	C
horse	cow	sheep
child	dog	man wearing hat
baby carriage	bicycle	hand-truck
mailbox	wooden gate	signpost
mailman	policeman	cat
garage	cafe	hotel
stream	lane	pond
tractor	barn	farm worker

A	B	C
school	post office	village shop
flower garden	vegetable garden	fruit trees
cart or wagon	churchyard	church tower
chestnut tree	elm	evergreen

Bingo Spy

Another spotting game while on the move — really a variation of *Seeing Things*.

This time let each player have a large square divided into nine small squares. The "things" can be taken from the preceding lists — a useful way of starting is for you to read all 36 items and allow players to put any they like in any squares they choose, so that no two papers will be alike. An example might be:

horse	cafe	pond
school	tractor	dog
barn	cow	hotel

Players watch their papers; one person looks out of the car or train window, and calls out things seen. Each time a player hears something which is on his paper, he crosses out that particular square — and when he gets three in line, *Bingo!* he has won.

Traffic Census

Play this when you are parked with traffic passing in both directions. One team, or individual, observes the passing cars on the near side of the road; the other watches those on the far side. Points are awarded according to the types of vehicle seen. Here is a possible table:

	Points
Small car	1
Large car	2
Station wagon	1
Small truck	1
Trailer truck	2
Bus	3
Motorcycle	4
Bicycle	3
Horse-drawn vehicle	6

Each team can have a scorer, or one person can score for the whole game. He will have a list of the various vehicles and will put down the score against each as it is called out by players.

A variant of the game can be planned by awarding different scores, according to the makes of car.

I Saw It

This is a slightly different form of *I SPY*, very popular with small children.

One child begins, having noticed something which you have just passed — for instance, a telegraph pole. "It was tall and thin," he says. "I just saw it."

Then the others begin to guess. If they fail, he can give a little more help: "It was black." When someone guesses right, he or she chooses the next thing.

Just Gone By

Here is a game for those boring moments in a stationary plane, or an airport lounge.

Make your list of things likely to be seen: man with hand luggage, woman with same, private car, fuel truck, uniformed pilot, hostess, mother with baby, policeman, passenger bus, bicycle, soldier, and so on. Players tell the scorer each time they spot any listed person or thing — and marks are awarded accordingly.

Alphabet Hunt

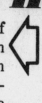

This is played with one or more youngsters on each side of the car. Players on the right look for letters they need on their side of the street or road, their opponents search on the left side. The presence of signs and lettering is obviously a necessary condition for play — there must be plenty of road signs, or you must be in a built-up area, traveling not too fast.

The aim is to spot each letter of the alphabet in its proper order, taking only one letter at a time from any particular sign board. The simplest method of play is to have the full alphabet written on paper and to cross off each letter as it is spotted. If you wish, one person can do all the scoring for both sides as the competitors call out their progressive letters.

License Letters

The leader calls out the three letters of a passing car's license plate, and competing players see who first can produce a word which includes these letters in their proper order, though not necessarily next to each other. For instance, NBD might be solved by *nabbed*, or WLE by *whale*.

Measuring Miles and Minutes

Miles, of course, are best measured on the road, while minutes can be tried anywhere. The leader will watch the roadside miles, or odometer, or keep his eyes on the second hand of a clock or watch.

Those competing have their eyes closed and try to judge when one mile (or one minute) has passed. There must be no speaking, but when a player judges that a mile has been traveled, he will raise his hand. The leader will note this, but will say nothing until all have made their signs. Then he will declare who was most accurate.

You may try for two miles — or two to five minutes. But insist on complete silence all the time.

Growing Numbers

Players take passing cars in turn, looking for pairs of numbers following in progressive order until the full range has been completed and there is a winner.

Numbers must be found in pairs, and they must be next to each other on the car plates, in correct order. The first two needed are 01 — a license plate with 107 would be of no use, but 801 would provide the necessary pair.

The growing numbers required are therefore: 01, 12, 23, 34, 45, 56, 67, 78, 89. And these must all be scored in their proper order.

Alphabet Spotting

Individuals, couples, or teams compete. Each has a paper with the letters of the alphabet written down one side, and tries to spot things beginning with each letter. You may want to eliminate X, Y, Z; Q, too.

Score as you please, depending on circumstances — the first to complete the list; the largest number of entries when you decide to call a halt; or the largest total. In the last case, individual points are scored for any number of items for each letter.

License Plate Spelling

The oncoming traffic needs to be right for this — plenty of cars, but not too many.

Each player selects a word; for small children it can be a simple one. The word is written down and then, watching the oncoming cars, each player picks his required letters from license plates, crossing out from his word each letter as he spots it.

The game can be made more difficult by ruling that the

letters must be seen in their proper order — ODG will not
do, it must be DOG. Still another variation, which lengthens the game, is for players to take the oncoming cars in
turn so that if three are taking part, each can score only
from every third car.

Color Car

Each player chooses a color, or alternatively, the colors are
written on slips of paper which the players draw.
    The game is simple, each player scoring one point every
time a car of "his" color goes by.

My Car

This is played like the preceding game, except that the
players look not for colors but for particular makes of car.

Car Bingo

Each player has a paper divided into nine squares and
writes any two-digit number he likes in each square. The
diagram shows the idea.

37	19	52
68	24	10
22	86	34

    Another person, who is not a player, simply observes the
license plates of passing vehicles and calls out pairs of
numbers as they appear.
    Players cross off their own numbers as they turn up, and
the first to get three in line — vertically, horizontally, or diagonally — wins. Players then draw new "bingo cards"
and are ready for a fresh round.

Odds and Evens

Here is a simple game for two children when there is little oncoming traffic.

One player looks for car plates ending with an even number, the other for those ending with an odd number. Alternatively, the beginning instead of the final numbers could be used. Let the children score their own points, or call out their claims while someone else does the scoring. Let "game" be 20 points, and begin a new game when one player has scored his 20.

▷2◁
Writing

Pencil and paper games are always popular. Here is a selection for all ages.

Alphabet Sentences

There are many possible variations of this game, some easy, some much more difficult, so that it can last minutes or hours. You can work individually, or several people can tackle it together.

One of the simplest ways is to choose a word at random — perhaps from the nearest newspaper or book — and then to construct a sentence in which each letter, in proper order, begins a word. For instance: LETTER — Let Ethel Try Toasting Edible Radishes (any sort of nonsense will do, provided it is a reasonable sentence); WHILE — We Hate Interfering Little Elephants.

A more difficult form is to use the whole alphabet, carrying on with one sentence as long as you can keep it going. Then begin another with the next letter — Ann Briefly Comes Down Every Friday. Geoffrey Hops In Jauntily. Kate Leaves Many Nice Oddments ...

It will be easier if your sentences are completely unrelated.

If you have plenty of time, try to get real continuity: Anybody can destroy eggs, flowers, gnats, herbs. I jokingly knocked little Magpie's nest over. Pitiful quavering rumpus, showed terrible upset. Very well — Xpand your zoos!

Stab

Draw a square not more than 1½ inches across. Divide this into nine smaller squares and in each square write the name of an animal, such as wolf, lion, bear, tiger, and so on.

bear	wolf	tiger
hyena	snake	hippo
rhino	jackal	lion

Two players at a time take part. One holds a pencil poised above the paper. The other calls out the name of one of the animals. Instantly, the one with the poised pencil must stab down upon the paper, hoping to hit the right square. If his stab is successful, he scores a point. Then the other player takes his turn.

You need not, of course, be restricted to animals. The squares could be filled with names of *towns, flowers, plants, birds, countries* — the choice is endless.

Make Your Own Limericks

Read out the first four lines of any limerick, then let the players have two minutes in which to produce a last line.

You may get your first parts from any limerick collection. Even if players know the originals, they may substitute last lines of their own devising. Here are a few, with the original endings.

There was a young girl of Quebec,
Who fell through the ice to her neck,
When they said: "Are you friz?"
She said: "Yes, course I is,
But we don't call this cold in Quebec."

There once was a girl of New York,
Whose body was lighter than cork,
She had to be fed
For six weeks upon lead,
Before she went out for a walk.

There was a young fellow from Lynn,
Who was so remarkably thin,
That when he essayed
To drink lemonade,
He slipped through the straw and fell in.

I Am A Poet

Each person has a numbered paper. Five minutes or so are allowed for each to write a four-line verse containing both the number and the player's name. Then all read their compositions in turn.

These examples will make clear the sort of thing that might be done:

My name is Smith,
My number, three.
So my task's as easy
As shelling a pea.

Well, Hetty is my name
(You wish you were the same?)
Yes, many think it's fine!
My number? Oh, it's nine.

Nine Spot

Each player writes down the figures 1 to 9 in square formation, as shown:

1   2   3

4   5   6

7   8   9

Then all begin together to solve the problem, and the one who first achieves the solution wins.

The requirement is to make a continuous pencil line, starting from 1, and joining up number after number, without ever crossing another line or running through another figure, and finally returning to 1. But after every new number the line must return to 1 before going on to the next number.

Of course it can be done, but it takes thought.

Endings

Agree on a certain subject. It may be anything from vegetables, animals, flowers or fruit, great men or women, buildings or towns.

Then one player suggests a letter of the alphabet, and all begin to write down names ending with that letter. If the subject is "colors," for instance, and the chosen letter is N, such words as *brown*, *green* and *crimson* could be put down. When everybody has finished, the lists are read out, each player scoring two points for a word which he alone has, and one point for a word duplicated by another player.

An alternative method of play is for each player to have a long list of subjects, and to write down words ending in the chosen letter for all of them. Considerably more time, of course, must be allowed for this.

Conglomeration

Each player writes the word "conglomeration" at the head of a sheet of paper, and has five minutes in which to write as many words as can be made from the letters of it — many more than most people expect!

Any other agreed long word can be used — for example, magistrate, nationality, generation, incomprehensible, or dependability.

Hidden Words

This is a variant of the previous game. Dictate a proverb, which everyone copies down. Then one minute is allowed in which all write the "hidden words" which they can discover, which must be formed from the letters of the proverb in their unaltered order.

Allow only letters which are next to each other.

Here is an example:

A rolling stone gathers no moss — roll, ling, in, ton, on, tone, one, at, the, her.

Beetle Drive

A beetle drive utilizes small tables with four people at each. But three or four players can have equal fun in the back of a car, or around any sort of makeshift table.

At such a table of four, the die is passed around and everybody takes one throw in turn.

Every player has a piece of paper, and on this the beetle must be drawn.

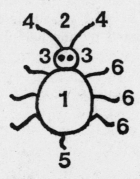

No drawing can be started until a 1 has been thrown with the die. The player who throws it draws the body of a beetle. No more can be drawn until a 2 is thrown, and then the head is added. To fill in the two eyes, two separate 3's must be thrown, then two 4's to complete the feelers. After a single 5, the tail may be drawn in, and a series of six 6's is needed for all the legs to be added.

The parts of the drawing must be added in proper order. It is of no use throwing a 5 for the tail before the head, eyes, and feelers have been drawn.

When any player has completed his drawing, he calls "Beetle!" The round is then over and all players total their scores, counting up the point values of the incomplete drawings.

For the next round, a different player has the first throw.

Transformations

Two words are chosen, both with the same number of letters, and the aim is to transform one into the other by changing one letter at a time and making a real word with each change.

For example, four can be transformed to five as follows — four, dour, door, moor, moon, morn, more, mire, dire, dive, five. And boy to man — boy, bay, ban, man. Words of five letters or more are naturally much more difficult to deal with, but solutions can generally be found. Black can become white by the following change — black, slack, stack, stark, stare, spare, spire, spine, shine, whine, white. The best list is always the one using the least number of words.

Rhyming Consequences

The aim of this game is to produce a number of four-line poems. It is advisable to suggest a meter at the outset. If, for instance, each player models his lines on "The way was long, the wind was cold," the results will be more amusing than might otherwise be anticipated.

The usual "consequences game" procedure is adopted — writing across the top, and folding down out of sight.

First, everyone writes an opening line, and this is folded down. The final word is rewritten below, so that for rhyming purposes it can be seen by the next player. The papers are passed one place along and a new line is added. This process is repeated until all four lines have been written.

Naturally, final products are varied. This would be a pretty good specimen:

> *The day was calm and on the sea*
> *The howling tempest frightened me*
> *They planted bean rows, one, two, three*
> *I do not like such poetry*

Journalism

Each player has three pieces of paper and is requested to write a question on one of them. These questions are then collected and mixed.

Next, every player writes down on his second slip a single word — his choice is absolutely unrestricted. These papers, too, are collected, and mixed in a separate pile.

Each person then receives one question and one word chosen from the piles, and is instructed to write on the third slip of paper an answer to the question, incorporating the single word, used grammatically.

A good deal of ingenuity is required when one is faced with such a problem as, "Why do seasick people turn green?" and it is necessary to include in the answer the word "relativity."

Answers should be short, and consist of not more than one sentence.

Geography

A letter is chosen — a good way to do this is to hand a book to any player, asking him to "find the second letter in the fifth word on page 89," or something of the sort.

The letter being announced, all begin to write down every geographical name they can think of beginning with that same letter.

After perhaps two minutes, the writing stops, and you take one paper and begin to read out the names on it. Everyone can then write down his own marks.

For a name which no one else has thought of, two marks are given; one mark for a name which several others have put down; and if a name has been included by *every* player, it is awarded no marks at all.

Each player in turn announces what points he has earned — and then another letter is chosen.

List Game

This is like Geography, but it is of more varied interest.

A sheet of paper is given to each player, down the left-hand side of which is written the following list — animal, mineral, vegetable, fruit, fish, flower, foreign town, country, river, mountain, author, book, king or queen, game, county or province, play, reptile, famous building, insect, bird, statesman or politician, singer, tool, god or goddess, artist. This list can, of course, be varied.

Then choose a letter, and allow everyone five or ten minutes — longer if you wish — to write down a name beginning with that letter for each item on the list.

At the end, one list is read and each player marks down his own points — two for each word that no one else has, one for any word which several other players thought of, none for every name which everyone has put down.

Then a new letter is chosen, and the game begins afresh.

Consequences

This old game is always popular, particularly if a new twist can be given to it. It is scarcely necessary to describe in detail how to play it — the strip of paper for each player; the single line of writing for each, carefully folded down and passed along; the fresh line of writing from the next player.

Here are some fresh variations:

Sport 1. An Olympic sport; 2. Description of event or trial; 3. Costume used on equipment; 4. Time or distance achieved.

The Book Review 1. Name of any book, preferably one popularly known; 2. Name of author, living or dead; 3. Extract from publisher's blurb. 4. Short review or comment on the book.

The Police Court 1. Name of the person arrested and brought for trial; 2. The subject of the charge; 3. What the defense stated; 4. What the judge remarked; 5. What the result was.

Mrs. New-Wife's Cookery 1. What her husband wanted for dinner; 2. The first ingredient she took; 3. The second ingredient; 4. The third ingredient; 5. How she cooked it; 6. What her husband said at dinner.

Nursery Rhymes ABC

Each player writes the letters of the alphabet down the left side of his paper and then tries to find a nursery rhyme beginning with each letter.

Name Names

Let the players decide on the name of a boy or girl, of about five letters, writing it down on the left side of a paper, one letter under the other. Then allow five minutes in which players must write down all the names they can think of beginning with the key letters. The winner will be the one who gets the most names.

Crosswords

Each player has a piece of paper marked into twenty-five small squares — five rows from side to side and five from top to bottom.

Each player in turn now calls out a letter, and everyone writes down this letter in any square he chooses. When twenty-five letters have been filled in, the winner is the player who can show most and longest complete words, either vertically or horizontally. One point should be counted for every letter of every word.

Rhymes to Order

Each player has a paper. Across the top of the paper every person writes two words which rhyme. Then the slip is folded over to hide the words, and passed on. Each person now writes two more rhyming words, without, of course, seeing those that are already on the paper. After this all the papers are gathered up and shuffled, and finally handed out again.

The game now really begins. Each player is required to write a verse, using as the last word in each of the four lines the words at the top of his slip of paper. Fair time should be allowed before the papers are collected and read — or read by the poets themselves.

The sort of awful results that can be expected may be judged from the following, in which the given words were: dig, big, crazy, lazy.

> "Fine exercise. You'd better dig,"
> Said Dad, "or you'll get lazy."
> "Oh, dear!" wailed Sam. "It's dreadful big;
> I'm sure 'twill send me crazy!"

Square Words

Draw a square measuring about two inches across. Divide this into sixteen small squares by putting three lines across each way at equal distances.

Now write across, in one of the rows, a word of four letters — anything you like. After that, add other letters and words until there is one letter in every square.

But here is the point — every line of four squares from left to right and from top to bottom must make a proper word or name. It will be like making your own crossword puzzle. Here is an example:

```
┌───┬───┬───┬───┐
│ T │ R │ I │ O │
├───┼───┼───┼───┤
│ R │ E │ N │ D │
├───┼───┼───┼───┤
│ A │ N │ N │ E │
├───┼───┼───┼───┤
│ M │ E │ S │ S │
└───┴───┴───┴───┘
```

Tick-Tack-Toe Numbers

This will keep your players busy for some time!

Each starts off with a tick-tack-toe diagram. Into this must be written the numbers 1 to 9 so that each line horizontally or vertically adds up to 15.

9	5	1
4	3	8
2	7	6

When that has been solved, try the still harder task of arranging the numbers so that the lines total 15, vertically, horizontally, and diagonally as well.

6	7	2
1	5	9
8	3	4

27

Talking

These can take little or lots of time, and can even be educational as well as amusing!

Snip

The players sit around and one tosses a balled-up handkerchief, or something, across to any other, at the same time calling a word of three letters, and immediately starts to count up to twelve, finishing "eleven, twelve, snip!" The one who received the toss tries, before "snip" is said, to reply with three words, each beginning with one of the letters of the original word in their proper order.

Thus, if "now" is called, the response might be "nuts, out, white."

When the reply is given in time, the successful player throws to someone else; but if he fails, and "snip" cuts him short, he falls out of the game. Thus, eventually, only one player is left.

Home Mechanic

Each person is required in turn to state a phrase describing some motoring or cycling mishap, and how it was dealt with — bringing in three words beginning with the same letter.

In order that players shall not know when their turn is coming, it is best that a balled-up handkerchief be tossed by the one who has just evolved his sentence, to anyone else. This next victim must deal with the next letter of the alphabet. Difficult letters such as k, q, x, z, should be omitted.

Here are examples:

My accelerator refused to act, so I amputated it.

My brakes were all broken, so I traveled by balloon.

My engine was exploding, but I've now educated it.

Packing for Vacation

Players must take turns in a definite order for this — and it gets more difficult the longer it goes on! Each player repeats what everybody has said before him, and adds some new thing, so that the farther around the play travels, the longer the list becomes.

The first player begins: "When I pack, I put in ..." and then he names whatever he likes — galoshes, for instance.

Then the second player goes on: "When I pack, I put in galoshes and an iron for taking creases out of sheets."

The third may continue: " — galoshes, an iron for taking creases out of the sheets, and some soap that really lathers."

Those going wrong may drop out of the game, or be marked down to pay some sort of forfeit afterward.

Alphabet Tail

In this the leader points to any player, at the same time giving a word which must be spelled correctly.

But the player who does the spelling has not finished when he has gone through the letters of his word correctly — he must continue with the rest of the alphabet, following from the last letter of the word.

Supposing, for example, the leader has called the word "scissors." The player pointed at will respond with the following letters: *scissorstuvwxyz*. There must be no pause, and the length of the "alphabet tail" naturally varies considerably, so that no one can be prepared in advance. With "zebra," of course, things are easy, since the entire alphabet follows.

Ads Needed

You will need to prepare for this. Have your list of words and then read them out to the players, one at a time, pausing until someone finds the correct solution for each.

Solutions can mean one point, and each player keeps his own score, until at the end the winner is determined.

The leader gives cryptic phrases, each indicating a word whose beginning is either "add" or "ad." He simply reads out sentences like the following:

Add that is risky (adventure)
Add that makes a fuss (ado)
Add that is youthful (adolescent)
Add that is quite near (adjoining)
Add that belongs to a letter (address)
Add that is related to a noun (adjective)
Add that is a dangerous reptile (adder)
Add that is an early school lesson (addition)
Add that is always in newspapers (advertisement)
Add that means farewell (adieu)

It is easy enough to build up a list of this sort from a dictionary.

Ants

Play as in the previous game except that the hidden syllable is "ant" instead of "add." The same method of play can be used — either points being scored, or successful players going to the head of the line.

Here are the examples — the dictionary will provide many more:

Ant that lived before the flood (antediluvian)
Ant that kills germs (antiseptic)
Ant that is very old (antique)
Ant that has collected passages of literature (anthology)
Ant that is fantastic (antic)
Ant that resembles goat and deer (antelope)

Ant that is far from the North Pole (antarctic)
Ant that has a strong dislike (antipathy)
Ant that is a kind of coal (anthracite)
Ant that is musical (anthem)

Tail Town

The players choose a leader. It is his task to set a time limit for each person in turn, by starting to count 20.

The first player begins by saying the name of any town. Instantly the leader begins to count his twenty. The second player must at once try to think of another town whose first letter is the same as the last of the town already given. This second name is called out and then the third player must get a name beginning with the new last letter. All who are counted out have a point scored against them.

Here are names as they might be given by the first ten players: Paris, Stockholm, Manchester, Rome, Exeter, Rio de Janeiro, Omsk, Khartoum, Mecca, Antwerp.

No name must be called twice. If the leader finds it difficult to get all the players out, he may reduce his counts to ten.

Tails and Legs

This is another form of the preceding game.

Only animals and objects having four legs can be mentioned, but the same rule of the last letter of one name forming the first of the next must be observed.

A list might run as follows: tiger, rat, table, elephant, trestle, ewe, elk, kid, dog, giraffe.

Alliteration

One player suggests a letter of the alphabet. Then each in turn, or any who volunteer, makes a sentence in which the same letter begins four words: a noun, a verb, an adverb, an adjective. These parts of speech can be in any order.

Here are a few examples:

The *sun shone steadily* through the *silent* hours.

The *bolts* are *boxed* and the *busy* workers load them *briskly*.

Alphabet Dinner

One starts off by saying: "I had today for dinner some asparagus (or something else beginning with A)."

The second player must repeat this, and add on something beginning with B; thus:

"I had today for dinner some asparagus and some beef." Each person in turn repeats the list of the previous player and lengthens it, alphabetically, by one item.

Later on, an unfortunate player might have to say something like the following:

"I had today for dinner some asparagus, beef, carrots, dates, eggs, French fries, grapes, hamburgers, Indian curry, jelly, ketchup, lentils, macaroni, nuts, oysters, plums, quince tart, red-currant tart, and some soup."

Any player who, when his turn comes, fails to repeat the full list or to make his new contribution to it, is out of the game.

Alphabet Jaunts

This is something like the preceding game, except that no one need repeat the full alphabetic list. To compensate for that, each player must this time think not merely of one, but three words beginning with the particular letter.

The game proceeds alphabetically, each player using his initial letter three times — one, for the name of a place; two, for a verb; three, for a noun. Here are some sample phrases:

I intend to go to Africa, to attack the alligators; to Bristol, to buy some beeswax; to Chicago, to collect camels; to Dublin, to dig for dinosaurs; to Everest, to examine the eagles; to France, to fix a fire-alarm.

One Awkward Albatross

This may be restful, physically, but it is a real brain-teaser.

The first player says:

"One awkward albatross."

His neighbor repeats this, but with an addition of his own — perhaps:

"One awkward albatross, two beautiful butterflies."

A third person may go on:

"One awkward albatross, two beautiful butterflies, three cute crocodiles."

So, as the game goes on, each player repeats the list, and adds the name of some new creature, together with some adjective, in alphabetical and numerical order.

Anyone who blunders drops out, until only the winner remains.

Rhymed Couplets

One player announces a first line, then any other, or each one in turn, makes an attempt to fit a rhyming second line. For example, to start,

"This game, I think, is not half bad."

And another player responds:

" 'Twould surely drive a poet mad."

Such rhymed couplets are easy to make, but there is much scope for wit and humor.

Where My Father Lives

This is a dialogue in which each player in turn shares. It might start as follows:

My father lives in Newtown where he deals in peaches.

Does he deal in plums?

No.

(Third player) Does he deal in cookies?

(First player) Yes!

The secret was that the father only dealt in things which had two-syllable names. The leader, or the next player, could restart, having in mind this time double letters within a word, as, for example:

My father deals in apples.

Does he deal in rope? (No) Sugar? (No) Buckets? (No) Mutton? (Yes).

Each time the "catch" can be different.

▷4◁
Thinking

Quick wits are needed here and there is plenty of amusement and fun for everybody.

Mother Magee

Turn to your left-hand neighbor and say:

"Mother Magee is coming to stay."

"What is she like?" asks your neighbor.

"She has her mouth wide open," you reply — and open your own.

The second player holds the same dialogue with his own neighbor, and so it passes around, until all are sitting with mouths wide open. Then your turn comes again, and this time you pass on the information that Mother Magee also has "her left eye shut," and soon each player has mouth open and left eye shut.

Something new is added for each round — and anyone who dares to smile is out of the game.

Quiz Race

If you have two children in the back of a car and you are driving, then this can pass the time pleasantly and even excitingly.

You simply call out: "Two boys, names beginning with P?" — and award a point to the first player who replies, "Percy, Patrick," or whatever. Then go on: "Two boys' names beginning with S." "Two girls' names beginning with G." "Two fruits' names beginning with C." "Two trees' names beginning with B." "Two games' names beginning with D." "Two countries' names beginning with E." The range is limitless.

Ghosts

One player starts off by saying any letter — having some word in mind beginning with that letter. His neighbor follows with a second letter, having also a word in mind of which these two letters form the beginning. The third follows on — and so on. The player who cannot follow, or who finishes a word, loses a "life."

Suppose the first player said "B" — thinking of *burn;* the second might add "R" — with *broken* in mind; the third could say "I," thinking of *bright;* and the fourth could add "M," thus finishing a word and losing a life.

The next player thereupon begins afresh with a new letter. So the game goes on without pause.

Anyone losing three lives becomes a "ghost." A ghost can speak to anyone; but anyone answering him becomes a ghost himself, and releases the previous ghost. Thus every ghost constantly tries to trap a player into speaking to him, in order that their roles may be reversed.

Proverbs

One player plugs his ears, while the rest decide on some proverb, apportioning one or more words of it to each player. Then the first person takes his fingers from his ears and asks whatever questions he likes, trying to discover the unknown proverb. Each person answering a question must include in it one of the words which has been given to him. For instance, if the proverb is, "Too many cooks spoil the broth," the first question might be, "Will you play ball tomorrow?" And the answer: "Yes, if rain doesn't spoil things."

Shopping

One player begins by saying, "I've been shopping."

"What did you buy?" asks the second.

"A jacket," responds the first.

Then the second player turns to another neighbor and says that he, too, has been shopping. In answer to the same query from this third player, the second tells him what he has bought — perhaps, a pencil.

The point is that players are allowed to have bought only things that they can actually touch without moving from their seats. There is plenty of fun in the game, and ingenuity will make it last a long time.

Of course, they need not know the secret at first, and you can award "right" or "wrong," according to whether they can really touch the thing mentioned.

Trades

This is another quick-thinking game in which one player acts as storyteller.

The others taking part each choose the occupation of a shopkeeper, and everyone has his own trade — grocer, baker, and so on.

The storyteller begins the tale — about a person who went shopping and visited a large number of tradesmen. Each time a shop is mentioned, he goes on to say that the shopper wanted to buy "something beginning with —" and puts in any letter of the alphabet. The player to whom this particular shop belongs must respond with something he is supposed to sell, beginning with this letter, before the storyteller can count ten. Failure to do so means that a point is scored against him.

As in all games of this sort, the more difficult letters like x, z, q, k, y, are best avoided.

If the shopkeeper cannot think of a suitable thing, anyone else is allowed to try during another count of ten, and if someone is successful, he is allowed to take away one point from any already scored against him.

Going Abroad

An alert and imaginative leader can bring a great deal of amusement into this game. He begins by saying that he is going abroad, and intends to take a certain thing with him. Each player successively makes a similar announcement, but chooses to take whatever thing he likes. Then the leader's turn comes again, and he informs the rest what he intends to do with his object. Everyone else must, in turn, declare that they intend to do precisely the same thing with the things they have chosen.

If there were six players, including the leader, the first two rounds of the game might go as follows:

I am going abroad and I shall take with me a pumpkin.

I am going abroad and I shall take with me a suitcase.

I am going abroad and I shall take with me a little dog.

I am going abroad and I shall take with me a lot of money.

I am going abroad and I shall take with me a diary.

I am going abroad and I shall take with me my passport.

I shall eat my pumpkin.

I shall eat my suitcase.

I shall eat the little dog.

I shall eat all my money.

I shall eat my diary.

I shall eat my passport.

The fun, of course, lies in the fact that no one knows what the leader intends to do until all the objects have been announced.

After the two rounds just described, the leader would start over again, saying that he was going abroad with something else. Each double round is quite complete, bearing no relation to what precedes or follows. You, as leader, might take a washcloth and boil it; a banana, and throw it into the sea; a cake, and cut it into little pieces.

Instant Rhymes

This instant rhyming is not easy, but it is good fun. You simply form couplets, impromptu, with as much sense in them as possible. The other players guess at the word you have in mind, to complete the second line. When someone calls it out, you improvise afresh. Here are examples:

> *I know a word that rhymes with flat,*
> *When on your head, you call it — (hat).*
> *I know a word that rhymes with fly,*
> *It isn't low, because it's — (high).*
> *I know a word that rhymes with slouch,*
> *If you are tired, then find a — (couch).*

You may have to repeat your couplet several times, minus the last word, while others are desperately trying to find the right conclusion. Incidentally, the best way to form your couplet is to make your first line, think of a possible final rhyming word, and then devise the second line which will lead up to this word.

A much simpler variant of this game is to use merely the rhyming words themselves. For instance, you think of *need* and *seed*, and tell the others your first word, *need*. They then begin to guess what the second word may be — read, reed, breed, lead, greed, bead, deed, weed, feed — and someone calls *seed*.

Superduper

One player plugs his ears so that he cannot hear the others decide on two words which have the same pronunciation, though different meanings — like *brake, break*.

The guessing player then unstops his ears and asks questions of the others until he discovers the words. Every reply made to him must be planned to contain the words, though instead of actually speaking them, "superduper" must be substituted.

Thus, supposing a question was:

"Are you going on a trip?"

The answer might be:

"Yes, in a car, but I hope the superduper does not superduper."

When at last the solution is found, another player plugs his ears.

This game is not as simple as it sounds and replies must be made as evasive and difficult as possible — a thing that may appear very obvious to one who has the key may be astonishingly troublesome for one without the slightest clue.

Chain

Something like *The House that Jack Built*, except that every sequence must be built up by the players. Everyone in turn adds a new link to the chain — but runs over the whole chain, too. If the whole company objects that any new link is unsatisfactory, the player concerned must immediately make another, or lose his place in the game, just as if he had failed to complete the entire chain.

Supposing the first player begins:

"I have the key of the deepest dungeon."

The second might continue:

"I have the ring that holds the key of the deepest dungeon."

The third could go on:

"I have the chain which holds the ring that holds the key of the deepest dungeon."

And the fourth might add:

"I have the belt that carries the chain which holds the ring that holds the key of the deepest dungeon."

The fifth's version could be:

"I have the jailer who wears the belt that carries the chain which holds the ring that holds the key of the deepest dungeon."

Thus the game will continue, and the chain will lengthen — one player after another dropping out as they make faults — until only the winner is left.

Fizz Buzz

Players begin to count, each following on in turn — 1, 2, 3, 4, and so on. But there is an important feature — neither fives nor sevens must be mentioned, nor any numbers of which they form part or into which they will go. In place of five, "fizz" must always be said, and "buzz" in place of seven.

The counting therefore goes as follows — 1, 2, 3, 4, fizz, 6, buzz, 8, 9, fizz, 11, 12, 13, buzz, fizz, 16, buzz, 18, 19, fizz, buzz, 22, 23, 24, fizz, 26, buzz, buzz, 29, fizz, 31, 32, 33, 34, fizz-buzz, 36, buzz, 38, 39, fizz.

When a player makes a mistake, a point is scored against him. The one with fewest such points at the end is the winner.

After fifty, the counting should be — fizz-1, fizz-2, fizz-3, fizz-4, fizz-fizz, fizz-buzz, fizz-buzz, fizz-8, fizz-9. After seventy, it will be buzz-1, and so on. When one hundred is reached, it is best to start afresh, or the counting may be taken backwards.

Sentences

It will be up to you as leader to think of words of not more than about six letters on which the others have to build sentences. You will also have to judge the sentences, and score the points.

When you have announced your word, each of the other people will try, in their own mind, to make a sentence in which each letter of the original word forms the initial letter of the complete word in its due order.

Here are some illustrations:

It — I'll try.

Bad — Baby annoyed Dad.

Able — Anyhow, Bill loves Ethel.

Brains — Be ready, as I now show.

Parties — Peggy asked Roger to illustrate each story.

The player who completes his sentence should at once raise his hand — and you will ask him to say it aloud. Should it be unsatisfactory, the next one to put up his hand is given his chance.

Earth, Air, Water

One player has a small object which he tosses to someone else, and at the same time he says — "earth," "air," or "water."

The player to whom the object has been thrown must try to mention some creature which lives in the element named before the first player can count ten. If he fails, he must throw to another person; but if he succeeds, the first player takes a fresh turn.

It would be wrong, of course, to say "tiger" when "water" had been called; but right to say "whale."

As in the preceding game, the briskness of the play has much to do with its enjoyment and success.

Europe, Asia, Africa

This is almost exactly like the preceding game, but instead, "Europe," "Asia," "Africa" are substituted and the response must be the name of some place or geographical feature in the continent referred to.

All Questions

This is for two players holding a dialogue, or for three or four, with each in turn replying to his neighbor. The point is that everyone must answer with a question, rather than any form of statement.

The conversation might run like this, with four players taking part: *First*, "Have we far to go now?" *Second*, "Do you think I know?" *Third*, "Didn't you say you did?" *Fourth*, "Is it fair to press him?" *First*, "Can anyone answer truthfully?" *Second*, "Of course, but — " "Out!" shout the others, and *Two* drops from the round.

It should be insisted upon that all the questions have some relevance to what has been asked by previous players.

Mixed Stars

Give to each player, or display to all, a jumbled string of letters, and from it see who can first discover the film or T.V. star whose name is thus mixed up.

One would hardly guess, at first glance, for instance, that e n h c r i c a l p a i l h were the jumbled letters of Charlie Chaplin.

How Shall We Go?

If you are on a long journey, you will have decided in advance on your route. If the children do not already know it, let each of them have a similar map so that they can work out a route for themselves — and see who gets nearest to the one you have chosen. Let them give reasons for their choice, and if they differ from yours, it is up to you to justify your own preference.

Ten Towns

If you have a similar map for each player, you can plan this game to suit the ability of those taking part.

Give to each the same list of ten towns, and see who first can find and put pencil rings around all of them.

I Remember Now

Mother, secretly, will have collected a dozen or so small things into a bag. When the children are ready, around a table, she tips them out. They remain on view for perhaps half a minute, then she sweeps them back into the bag.

Let each player write down a list of things, and see who can remember all.

Instant Memory

A pack of cards is spread out on the "table," face downward. Each player in turn turns over two cards, for just an instant, so that all can see them. If the two form a pair, he takes them. The point of the game lies in remembering the cards that have been turned up and replaced, so that, having lifted any card, you know where to turn up its fellow. The winners are, of course, the players who get most pairs. Having taken a pair, a player is allowed to turn up two more, and to continue until he shows two odd ones.

Birds, Animals

Those letter cards used for many spelling and other games are needed for this. Put a pile of them, letter-side down, in the middle of the "table."

The first player now draws a letter at random and places it face up in front of him. All the players try to think of the name of an animal or bird beginning with that letter. The first person who is successful takes the card. If no one can think of a name, the card remains down. Then the second player draws another letter, and the same thing is repeated. After a full round, those cards which have not been claimed are put back in the middle of the table, and the new round begins. The winner of the game is the player who finally has most cards.

No name must be used more than once.

⇨5⇦
Drawing

The quality of work will naturally vary according to the artist. But "art" is a loose sort of term when applied to the following games!

Travel Picture

The bumpier the road, or the car, the better the game.

Have drawing paper in front of you and hold the point of your pencil down on it. Let the jolts of the car move the pencil. After a sufficient time, examine the wriggly lines and see if you can make them into some intelligible picture or design.

Picture Consequences

This is played in ordinary *Consequences* fashion, but pieces of paper should be ten or twelve inches long.

To begin, each player draws some picture — anything he likes. Papers are then passed to neighbors, and each person looks at the picture he has received, and writes underneath a title for it, describing what he thinks it to be. The top of the paper is now folded over so that the picture is covered, but the title can be seen, and all pass on once more. This time players draw pictures again, illustrating the titles. After the next change, new titles are given to these pictures. Then new pictures are drawn for these titles, and so on.

When all have finished, or papers are filled, each can unfold the slip he has, and the collection slowly passed around for inspection.

Famous Events

Each player sets to work to draw some "famous events." The resulting pictures are displayed, and those successfully guessed by the greatest number are declared the winners.

Each "picture" should be signed by the "artist."

Whose Zoo?

Give each player a slip of paper. Each one writes the name of some animal or other living creature across the top of it. The top is then folded down to cover the writing and the slip is passed on — as in *Consequences*. Again players write down the names of other living creatures, and pass on the papers after once more folding them. This process is repeated twice more. Then the slips are collected, shuffled, and handed out again.

Each player thus finds himself with a paper on which are written the names of four living things. He must then set to work and draw a creature incorporating the characteristic appearances of all four things.

It is not easy to draw a creature featuring toad, lion, weasel, and rabbit!

Heads, Bodies and Legs

Here is another combination of drawing and *Consequences*.

This time each player helps to draw a human being.

The first thing is to draw the head. This is folded down so that only the two ends of the neck show. To these the next player will add shoulders. The next will add arms and trunk; and the fourth, legs; the fifth and last, feet.

Then papers are unfolded, and an "exhibition" of finished drawings is held.

Line Designing

Each player makes a single bold line across his piece of paper. The line may be of any shape.

Then papers are passed on, and each person tries to make a drawing or design based on the line which he now has. Any sort of picture will do, provided the original line is a central feature.

Academy

Players are numbered one to four — each has pencil and paper. The *one* is instructed to draw a triangle, *two* a square, *three* a circle, *four* a cross. Each figure should measure about three inches across.

Now, on these foundations, fuller drawings are to be made.

Each triangle must be made into a house, each square into a face, each circle into an animal, each cross into anything the artist may choose.

Five or ten minutes can be allowed. Then drawings are signed and passed around for all to see. Have four rounds so that each player can try each basic figure.

Star Maps

Each player puts six large dots on his paper, representing stars. They can be scattered anywhere.

Papers are then passed on to neighbors, and each person joins these stars into some figure and writes at the bottom the name of the "new constellation" which it represents.

Dot Designs

This is like the preceding game — half a dozen dots are scattered over each paper — but any picture or design can be based on these dots instead of merely a star constellation.

Sometimes, for a change, you may settle at the beginning that one dot must be an eye, or the corner of a house, or the wing tip of an airplane. This will make your task more difficult, but more interesting, too.

◇6◇
Puzzling

Some quiet brain-teasers to be worked out individually.

Four to Three

Place twelve matches so as to form one large and four small squares, as shown in the diagram. The problem is to take away four matches and replace them in such a way as to leave three squares.

It is easy enough when you see the solution here, but you won't let the other players see this page!

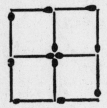 

Match Square

Form a large square with three matches for each side, and divide this into nine small squares by putting two rows of three matches across each way. You thus have three rows of three squares, counting either up and down or side by side.

The problem is to take away exactly eight matches and to leave two squares.

You will find it not a bit easy — until you know the secret. Simply remove the two matches forming the inner sides of each of the four corner squares. This will leave you with the one center square, and the large outer square enclosing it.

Where nearly everyone gets tripped up is in expecting to leave two small squares of the same size.

Giant to Dwarf

Get nine pieces of cardboard of distinct and graduated sizes. It is easy enough to get all nine quite different if you have a very small one at one extreme and a really large one at the other. They can be square, but it is better to have them round.

Put these nine counters down, without regard to size, in three straight columns of three, just a few inches apart. Your problem is to get all nine into a single column, with sizes in proper order — largest at the top, smallest at the bottom.

Start off, then. You can move only one counter at a time, and only from the bottom of one column to the bottom of another. And — this is the important thing — a counter can only be put under one of a larger size.

Often, of course, one of the three columns is completely cleared, and later on replaced for the time being with fresh counters. When a column is empty, any counter which you have can be placed at the head of it, as the rule about having a bigger counter above cannot apply.

In your first attempts, you will often think that you are hopelessly jammed, but experience will soon show you that there is always a way out.

Instead of having counters of graduated sizes, you may have them all the same size, but numbered, so that the numbers serve in place of the varying sizes. Or, of course, ordinary playing cards can serve. However much you play the game, it will always be fresh and different, for you will never solve it twice in quite the same way, because the three columns will always be different when you lay them out for a new start.

Penny Puzzle

This little coin trick requires four pennies. They should be laid on a table, thus:

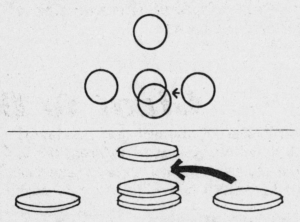

Ask your companions to rearrange the coins with a single move so that there are two rows with three in each.

The thing is done by putting one of the end pennies, of the row of three, on top of the middle coin of this same row.

Matchbox Magic

This is a simple, impressive trick. The only preparation you need is a matchbox containing a few matches fastened flat against your wrist, just far enough up your arm to be securely covered by your sleeve. The box should be on the left wrist.

Now, you empty a matchbox on the table, and close this box again, declaring that you are going to make matches come back into it. After shaking it with the right hand, when it gives, of course, no sound, make a "magic pass" above it with this same hand, then pick it up with the left hand. Shake it again and this time there will be the distinct rattle of matches — from the concealed box, though to the spectators the sound will seem to come from the box in the hand. You put down the box once more; make a new pass over it; shake it in the right hand, and there is no sound — the contents have been spirited away.

A trick of this sort should not be repeated too many times.

Match Maths

Here are a few simple puzzles, depending just on Roman numerals. The simplest way of demonstrating the solutions is to put down matches to form the letters. But don't show off all the problems at one time, because once the Roman key is understood, all the problems immediately become simple.

    a. Take three matches and with them make four (IV).

    b. Make three matches into six, without breaking them or splitting them (VI).

    c. With only two matches make five (V).

    d. With eight matches make twenty seven (XXVII).

    e. Take one match from nine and leave ten (IX, X).

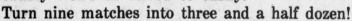

Multiplying Matches

This sounds much more impressive than the last trick, and probably won't be solved so easily:

    Turn nine matches into three and a half dozen!

    Well, first put three of the matches into a little pile, and six into another pile. You have three — and a half-dozen.

Seven Points

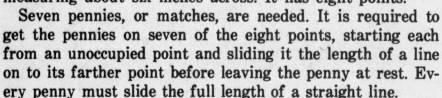

Each person tries this problem in turn. Draw the diagram measuring about six inches across. It has eight points.

    Seven pennies, or matches, are needed. It is required to get the pennies on seven of the eight points, starting each from an unoccupied point and sliding it the length of a line on to its farther point before leaving the penny at rest. Every penny must slide the full length of a straight line.

    This is not easy, until the secret is known, and most players at first will be hard pressed to get five or six in place.

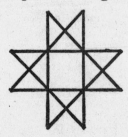

The secret lies in filling the second end of each line in turn. Each point, of course, is the junction of two lines, so that the penny on the second end of one line automatically becomes the first penny on another line. Thus the next move is to complete this second line, which consequently begins a third line — and so on.

Elimination

A checkerboard is used for this.

Put men on all the white squares of the board, except one — you can leave the vacant square anywhere you like.

It is not necessary to know anything about playing checkers, apart from how to jump and remove the man which has been jumped.

That is what you now do. Continue jumping over, one man at a time, and removing the men until — if you have completely succeeded — only a single man remains on the board.

But it isn't likely that you will often achieve that!

Remember that you can jump in any direction, just as a king does in the ordinary game. You will find that, although a lot depends upon which square is left empty at the start, it is still more important to aim all through at keeping the remaining men close together.

▷7◁
Guessing

Here are some simple and relaxing games that need practically no brain-power!

Open It

The players form two parties, two or four in each, and sit on opposite sides of some sort of table. A nut, button, or something small, is given to one team, and the players of that side put their hands under the table and pass the object along, eventually settling to leave it in one hand. Then they all put their closed fists up on the table, fingertips underneath, and those on the other side try to guess which hand holds the object.

If a hand is thought to be empty, the order, "Take it away" is given, and the hand is removed from the table. Or "Open it" can be called, upon which the hand must immediately open.

Should the object be found, the guessing team takes it, shuffling it between themselves under the table. But if they make a mistake, ordering the wrong hand to open, or the right one to be taken away, then the first team wins the game and has another turn.

Call Your Card

Deal the cards to those taking part as you sit around your "table." None must look at his own card. Each in turn places one card face upward in the middle, but before he plays it he must call out what he thinks it will be — spade, club, diamond, heart. If he is right, he takes all those in the center pile.

The winner is the one with most cards at the end of play.

Mystery Spell

One player leads; the rest sit around, each having five dried peas. The leader thinks of any word of about six letters; it is sensible for him to write it down for his own convenience.

Then each player in turn takes a guess at the letters of the word, one letter at a time. If a suggested letter is in the word, the player gives one pea to the leader, and the letter is crossed off in the written word. Should a suggested letter not be in the word, it is the turn of the next player to take a guess. At any time a player may guess at the whole word — for a right guess, he becomes leader; for a wrong one, he is compelled to receive three peas.

The first player to reduce his peas to one immediately becomes leader and starts a new word. All the other players start anew with five peas.

Crossed Scissors

A pair of scissors is passed from one to another player until everyone has discovered the secret of the game.

Each time that a player passes on the scissors, he says either "I pass them crossed" or "I pass them uncrossed" — and the leader, or those who already know the game, declare instantly whether that is "right" or "wrong."

The secret does not depend at all on whether the scissors themselves are open or closed, or even on the way the words are spoken. Everything rests on the position of the hands. The hands or wrists must always be crossed or uncrossed to fit whichever word is spoken — though it takes a long time for many players to discover that the scissors themselves are of no account.

He Can Do Little

This is a game similar in principle to Crossed Scissors.

The players sit around a "table." You hold a pencil in your right hand, and you proceed to tap the point of it on the "table," at the same time saying.

"He can do little who cannot do this."

Immediately you pass the pencil to your left-hand neighbor, and he will endeavor to repeat the same performance. As he, in turn, hands on the pencil to the third player, you will declare whether he has been "right" or "wrong." So it passes around, and the unobservant ones will almost certainly fail, and probably many of the ordinarily observant ones, too.

At the outset, you will have been looking down at the point of the pencil and will have knocked with vigor and marked rhythm. Consequently, nearly everyone will be giving their chief attention to this tapping, probably trying to fit it in with the words. Actually, the secret lies in something quite different — each player must hold the pencil in his right hand while tapping, but take it into his left hand in order to pass it on to his neighbor. The common blunder is to pass it on with the right hand, which already has it.

Peas Please (or Matches)

Several players take part and to each is given the same number of dried peas, or matches. If four are taking part, let each have six or seven peas — there must be more than the number of players.

The starting player holds out his clenched hand, in which lie concealed as many peas as he likes. The other three players guess in turn how many are in the fist. If a guess is right, the first player must give one pea to each of the others; if all are wrong, each of them must give one pea to him. Play goes on until individuals are eliminated, with no peas left, or until you decide to count and determine winners by the number of peas held.

Coin Cunning

To work this little trick, you must make quite sure of the ~~f~~llowing phrase:

"I will make the number odd if it is even, and even if it is odd."

All you have to do is to invite any person to draw a few coins from pocket or handbag, and count them, without letting you see. Then, you declare, you will be able to give a suitable number of other coins, which will "make the number odd if it is even, and even if it is odd."

Don't let them think much about it, for the thing is rather absurdly simple — you simply give an odd number of coins.

What I Like

The leader decides, of course without telling the others, on a certain letter which is taboo — it is best to have a vowel. Perhaps he settles for A. He might then begin by saying: "I like onions." Each will follow in turn and will be told "Yes" or "No" by the leader. The second player could say: "I like roses." "Okay," responds the leader. The third player follows with: "I like journeys." Leader: "Yes!" Fourth player: "I like dahlias." The leader shakes his head — it won't do.

What Is It?

This simplified variant of the familiar old game *Twenty Questions* can be played in train, car, plane — anywhere.

The leader simply thinks of any object in the world, and the others must find what it is by continuing questions. But the only replies they get to their questions are Yes or No.

They may be trying to discover: Tom's right thumb, or the last snowflake to fall on the top of Mount Everest, or the whiskers on a pet cat.

8
Competing

Many games involve competition, but in some of these the competition can become fierce.

My Box

First make a square of perhaps 36 dots — the diagram shows how.

Two or three players can take part. Each in turn draws a short line between two adjacent dots, anywhere on the diagram. The aim of a player is to add the fourth line which will complete any small square. When he achieves this, he puts his initial into the square. At the end of play, that player having the most "signed boxes" is the winner.

You will naturally try not to add a third line to any growing square, for when you do the next player will immediately add the required fourth and so secure the box.

Tick-Tack-Toe Marathon

Two players take part. Instead of the usual tick-tack-toe diagram, they use 25 "boxes," formed by four horizontal and vertical lines.

Play proceeds as in the familiar old game, the first player putting in his noughts one at a time, wherever he pleases, and the other putting in his crosses. The aim of each is to get as many threes in a row as possible, and of course to prevent his opponent from doing the same. A three may be counted horizontally, vertically, or diagonally, but no nought or cross can be counted twice. Thus, if there is a straight line of five crosses it can only count as one *three*.

The diagram shows the completion of a game. In it the noughts have scored three, and the crosses four.

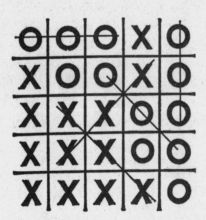

To Berlin

Draw a large circle around a dinner plate laid on a piece of paper. Put three lines across, through the center, dividing the circle into six approximately equal divisions. In each section write one of the following names — Rome, Paris, London, Antwerp, Brussels, Barcelona. At the middle draw a small circle, around a wooden spool, and inside this write Berlin.

Two or more players can now take part. Each in turn poises his pencil over the target, which lies flat on the table; closes his eyes; makes three circling sweeps with the raised hand — then brings the point of the pencil down on the paper. If the pencil descends on any of the large sections, as many points are scored as there are letters in the city name of that section. The first player to reach a total of 100 wins the game. But if the pencil falls into the Berlin area, the game is won immediately.

Slap the Jack

The several players sit around your "table" with the pack of cards shuffled and placed face down at the center. Each in turn takes the top card from the pile, placing it face up in a second pile at the center. Whenever a Jack appears, the players immediately clap their hands three times and then try to "slap the Jack"; the first to touch it takes the whole of the face-up pile for himself. So the game continues until all the Jacks have been shown and won. The last winner takes the remaining cards from the center.

The round is won, of course, by the player who has acquired the most cards.

Please, Thank You

When the cards are dealt around, each player checks to see if he has any sets of four cards of each suit, such as four Aces, four Tens, and so on. Any such sets of four must be put face downward in front of him, so none know what they are. The player on the left of the dealer can then turn to any other player, saying: "Please, Jim, or Jane),may I have a King (or Five of Hearts, or any specific card)." The caller must, however, hold at least one card of the set when he asks — his concern being to complete his set. If the player asked has the required card, he must at once hand it over, and the recipient must say: "Thank you." The recipient is then free to make the same request to any other player. Should the player asked not have the card, he must say: "Sorry," and is then entitled to ask for any card which he himself wants. If he fails to say, "Sorry," he forfeits this chance and the previous player continues with a new request.

If any asking player fails to say "Please" or "Thank you," he loses his right to make another request. Play continues until someone wins by completing all his sets.

Old Maid

Three or more players take part in this. But first remove three Queens from the pack, the fourth (remaining) one to be designated the Old Maid.

When the cards have been dealt around, each player discards, to the center of the "table," any pairs he may have (two Kings, two Sixes, etc.). Now the play begins, the leader proffering his hand of cards face downward to the player on his left — who takes any single card. If with this card the second player is able to make a new pair for himself, the pair must be laid on the center pile and he himself will proffer his own hand to his left-hand neighbor. If a card taken will not match another, the player who received it simply adds it to those he already has in hand.

So play continues until everyone has discarded all his pairs — and the loser remains with the single Old Maid.

Losing Checkers

For a quick, interesting game with the usual checkerboard and men, try this.

It is a reversal of the ordinary style. Instead of trying to retain your men, you "give them away" to your opponent as quickly as you can — and the player who first loses every man becomes the winner.

The customary rules concerning captures and kings remain in force, except that you do your utmost to compel your opponent to get *his* men crowned!

Fox and Geese

This also is an amusing game that is played on a checkerboard.

One player has only one man — the fox; and his opponent four men — the geese. Each side starts from the back line, at opposite sides of the board. If the fox succeeds in breaking through the line of geese, he wins; but he loses if they manage to pen him up so that no further move is possible to him. There is no capturing and removing of pieces.

All the men move diagonally, as in checkers, one square at a time, without any exceptions whatever. But while the geese are allowed to go forward only, the fox can move backward as well.

Lone Wolf

This resembles the previous game, but no diagonal moves are permitted. The checkers move only vertically or horizontally, backward or forward, one square at a time, except when jumping, in these same straight lines.

One square at a corner of the board is termed the *lair*. In the diagonally opposite corner is a black checker, the *lone wolf*, whose aim it is to get safely into his lair. Trying to prevent him, by capture, is the *pack* — three white checkers which at the beginning of the game are in the three squares immediately adjoining the lair.

So play begins. The *loner* can jump any of the pack if he has a chance, and any of the *pack* may jump the *wolf*, thus ending the game. The *loner* wins if he gets into his lair.

Latrunculi

The Roman latrunculi (bandits) is the earliest form of checkers known. It can be played on a board or pencilled diagram containing only sixteen squares — a quarter of an ordinary board will serve. Each player has four men lined along his back row at the start, and play begins in ordinary fashion with single, forward diagonal moves. Every square of the board can be played on and captures are made just as in the

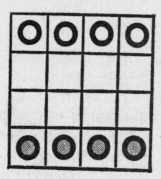

modern game. When a man reaches the back line of his opponent's side, he takes on the power of a king, being allowed to move backward as well as forward.

Of course, the scope in this game is rather restricted, but the novelty of having every square available for play makes it interesting.

Kings

Here is an interesting adaptation of the end game of ordinary checkers.

Each player has four kings set along his rear line. They have their usual power of moving one square at a time, diagonally, either backward or forward, and the play proceeds in the familiar way.

A good deal of fun can be obtained by a four-handed game of kings. In this, one player sits at each side of the board, and each has three kings. Players can act quite independently or in couples, those facing each other combining.

In four-handed games, each player in turn around the board should take his move. It is necessary also that four distinct sets of men are used — if you don't have different colors, you may get the distinction by having odd sizes.

Daama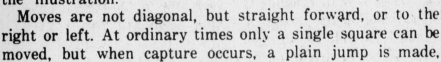

This Turkish game of Daama (Queen) is quite a change from any so far described. All sixty-four squares of the board are used, and each player has sixteen pieces. These are placed, at the beginning, across the second and third rows of the board, counting from the back — as shown in the illustration.

Moves are not diagonal, but straight forward, or to the right or left. At ordinary times only a single square can be moved, but when capture occurs, a plain jump is made,

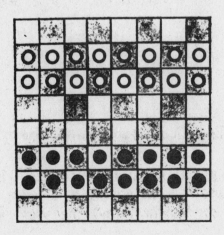

though not diagonally. When a piece wins through to the rear line, it becomes a Daama, and is crowned. The Daama can move any number of squares, like the rook in chess, and can capture at any distance, provided the square on the far side of the attacked piece is vacant for the Daama to alight upon.

When a piece has reached the crown line, the opposing player must make one move before the Daama is allowed to leave the square. A Daama can be captured just like ordinary pieces.

Five In a Row

One player has five white checkers, the other five black. Each in turn puts down one man, until all are down. The aim is to get your five men next to each other in a straight row, diagonally, vertically, or horizontally. If all the men are down and neither player has yet succeeded, the checkers can be moved about one square at a time until a win is achieved.

It is a sort of complicated tick-tack-toe, without the bother of drawing new diagrams all the time.

Eight Independents

All you must do — though it is not so simple — is to put down eight checkers on the board, so that there are never two in the same line, diagonally, vertically, or horizontally.

There are a number of varied solutions. One is shown in the diagram.

Just start by putting the eight checkers down one at a time. If, as is likely, your last one or two cannot find the requisitely clear squares, put them down anyhow, and continue to move your checkers around the board until a solution is found.

9
Singing

You can sing anything, from the current favorites to nursery rhymes, familiar old rounds or folk songs. Here are some other ideas!

Nursery Rhyme Mimes

There is plenty of fun to be had from miming or dramatizing familiar rhymes — without moving from your seat. You can all sing together, each improvising actions at will. Or sing solo. Or one person can just mime the rhyme without any singing and let the rest try to guess what the rhyme was.

You might have:

*The king was in his counting house, counting
out his money,*
    (hands busy with piles of gold)
*The Queen was in her parlor, eating bread and
honey,*
    (spreading and eating very delicately)
*The maid was in the garden, hanging out the
clothes,*
    (from basket to clothesline)
*When down came a blackbird and pecked off
her nose.*
      (with a fierce swoop of the hand,
        and a frightful snip)

Alphabet Singsong

See if you all can keep a singsong going, beginning each separate item with the appropriate letter of the alphabet: *All things bright and beautiful, Blow the man down, Clementine, Diane.* Of course you will doubtless include some from the current favorites.

Skip Syllables

Starting all together on the opening of the first word of any song, you will proceed to go through it, omitting every other syllable. There should thus be alternate gaps and the spoken syllables, and most humorous effects come from players who blurt out at moments that should be silent.

As an illustration, this is how Clementine would be sung:

Oh——darl——, Oh——darl——,
Oh——darl——, Oh——darl——,
Clem——tine,
——are——and——for——er,
——ful——ry, ——en——.

Any song can be treated — or maltreated — in this way; but try fairly slow ones until your singers have had some practice.

⇨10⇦
Exercising

Here are some "sitting-still" exercises that can help to ease cramped muscles, as well as being fun.

Film Faces

This is a "screen test." You must see that each aspirant is in full view of all the rest, then you will whisper to him some expression which you want his face to register. He will contort his features in the manner he thinks most suitable — and then the others will try to guess what it is he is depicting.

Here are some suggestions:

Scorn, love, hate, jealousy, pride, awe, suppressed merriment, indigestion, terror, conceit, loathing, sympathy, disappointment, victory, defeat.

This Is My Nose

Here is a game that can be relied on to set everyone laughing. Let one start off by touching his nose with one hand and pointing to any player with his other, at the same time saying:

"This is my ear."

That player who has received the information may repeat the foolishness while pointing at still another person; or he may touch his ear, exclaiming:

"This is my nose."

Words and action must always be contradictory, and the game should be played very briskly.

Finger Hug

Hold your little finger straight and stiff, and then pass its longer neighbor around behind, sliding it down until it encircles the small finger's lowest joint.

A good many people fail completely to make the third finger go of itself even behind its fellow.

Any practiced violinist can do this quite easily with his left hand, though not necessarily with his right.

Middle Finger Waggle

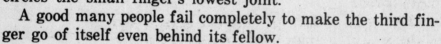

Hold one hand out in front of you, quite flat, with fingers and thumb straight and together. Now spread the thumb and its neighbor, the first finger, as widely apart from the rest as possible, by moving them sideways. Throughout the test be careful to keep these two touching and with their positions unchanged. The third and fourth fingers will also touch each other and be pressed well to the side. Also, the hand must remain always flat.

The middle, or second, finger must now move by itself from side to side, keeping quite straight, and so touching the first and third finger in turn.

People whose fingers are not limber enough for this feat find that the thumb and first, like the third and fourth, always separate when the second tries to move.

Crosswires

Each person in turn tries to do a simple little feat several times in succession.

Suppose you start off — to show the others how the thing is to be done. You grip your nose with your left hand, and your left ear with your right hand. Then, as someone calls "Change!" you release your holds; clap your hands once; and change your grips — right hand to nose, left hand to the right ear. "Change!" is called again. You clap; reverse once more — and so on.

Then let the next person try.

The thing should go briskly. But let only one person at a time try, so that the rest may enjoy being spectators before their own turn to perform comes around.

One, Two

This is an "exercise game," the actions and movements of which will depend on the space available and how wedged-in the players are.

The first player performs some action, like clapping hands in front of him, twice; the next repeats this "one-two" and adds something else — perhaps stamping right foot, then left foot. The third claps, stamps — and nods his head twice. The steady one-two rhythm should be maintained all through, and the play can continue as long as new movements are thought up.